★
THE
BIG
TIME

ANDREW LUCK

LAURA K. MURRAY

CREATIVE  EDUCATION

ANDREW LUCK

TABLE OF CONTENTS

MEET ANDREW

The game clock ticks down. Andrew looks down the field. His teammate runs to get open. Andrew pulls back the football and throws a long pass. Touchdown!

Andrew Luck is a professional football player. He plays for the Indianapolis Colts in the National Football League (NFL). Many people think he is one of the best quarterbacks today.

The Colts belong to the American Football Conference (AFC) South division.

ANDREW'S CHILDHOOD

Andrew was born September 12, 1989, in Washington, D.C. He has two younger sisters and a brother. As a child, Andrew lived in England and Germany. The Lucks moved to Texas when Andrew was 11.

Andrew with his mom, sisters, and NFL commissioner Roger Goodell in 2012.

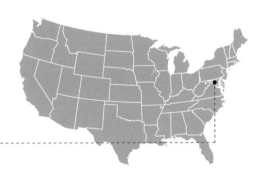

WASHINGTON, D.C.

GETTING INTO FOOTBALL

Andrew's dad had played pro football. But he wanted Andrew to do whatever made him happy. Andrew played youth football in Texas. Then he became a star for his high school team.

Andrew's dad enjoyed watching his son play high school football.

Andrew decided to play college football for Stanford University. He threw 82 touchdowns for Stanford! Andrew set lots of school records. He won awards for being the best college football player.

Andrew was the runner-up for the Heisman Trophy in 2010 and 2011.

THE BIG TIME

Many people thought Andrew would leave college to join the NFL. But he got his degree first. Andrew was the top overall pick in the 2012 *NFL Draft*. The India-napolis Colts chose him to be their new quarterback.

....

Andrew is 6-foot-4 and weighs 240 pounds.

Andrew broke NFL passing records as a *rookie*. He played in the ***Pro Bowl*** for three straight years! In 2014, he threw 40 touchdowns. That was the most in the NFL. The Colts almost made it to the Super Bowl.

....

Andrew celebrates a touchdown in the end zone.

OFF THE FIELD

When he is not playing football, Andrew loves watching soccer. He spends time with his family. He likes going to concerts and playing board games, too.

. . . .

Andrew teaches kids about healthy habits at an NFL Play 60 event.

WHAT IS NEXT?

Andrew helped the Colts make the playoffs in 2012, 2013, and 2014. He got hurt and missed a lot of games in 2015. Still, fans hoped Andrew would play in the Super Bowl soon!

In the 2014 season, Andrew and the Colts won their division.

WHAT ANDREW SAYS ABOUT ...

GOING PRO

"It's a job.... You owe the fans, you owe the owner, you owe the coaches, you owe your teammates a professional manner of work."

MAKING MISTAKES

"Everybody is gonna make mistakes, you're going to have failure along the way, but bouncing back is, I think, important."

NOT WINNING AWARDS

"In the NFL it's great to win, as it's a competitive culture, ... but I wouldn't want to do things differently or wish I could go back."

GLOSSARY

NFL Draft the yearly event in which NFL teams choose players

Pro Bowl a football game in which the best players in the NFL play against one another

rookie a player in his first season

WEBSITES

Andrew Luck

http://www.colts.com/team/roster/andrew-luck/ea912f8f-b6a5-4782-8b64-835b8fd58805/

This site has information on Andrew's life and career, including photos.

Andrew Luck Profile

http://www.nfl.com/player/andrewluck/2533031/profile

Check out Andrew's game and career stats.

READ MORE

Frisch, Aaron. *Indianapolis Colts*. Mankato, Minn.: Creative Education, 2014.

Gregory, Josh. *Andrew Luck*. New York: Bearport, 2014.

INDEX

PUBLISHED BY Creative Education
P.O. Box 227, Mankato, Minnesota 56002
Creative Education is an imprint of The Creative Company
www.thecreativecompany.us

DESIGN AND PRODUCTION BY Christine Vanderbeek
ART DIRECTION BY Rita Marshall
PRINTED IN the United States of America

PHOTOGRAPHS BY Corbis (Jonathan Bachman/AP, Charles Baus/NewSport, Julio Cortez/AP, Tony Dejak/AP, Joe Mahoney/AP, Andrew Mills/Star Ledger, Cliff Owen/AP, Gene J. Puskar/AP, David Richard/AP, Tim Sharp/AP, SHANNON STAPLETON/Reuters, TMB/Icon SMI), iStockphoto (AnthiaCumming, Pingebat), Newscom (John Albright/Icon SMI)

LIBRARY OF CONGRESS CATALOGING-IN-PUBLICATION DATA
Murray, Laura K.
Andrew Luck / Laura K. Murray.
p. cm. — (The big time)
Includes index.
Summary: An elementary introduction to the life, work, and popularity of Andrew Luck, a professional football quarterback star who broke rookie NFL records with the Indianapolis Colts.

ISBN 978-1-60818-668-6 (HARDCOVER)
ISBN 978-1-56660-704-9 (EBOOK)
1. Luck, Andrew, 1989–. 2. Football Players—Biography. 3. Quarterbacks (Football)—Biography. I. Title.
GV939.L81M87 2016
796.332092—dc23 [B]   2015026252

CCSS: RI.1.1, 2, 3, 4, 5, 6, 7; RI.2.1, 2, 5, 6, 7; RI.3.1, 5, 7, 8; RI.4.3, 5; RF.1.1, 3, 4; RF.2.3, 4

FIRST EDITION 9 8 7 6 5 4 3 2 1

Note: Every effort has been made to ensure that the websites listed above are suitable for children, that they have educational value, and that they contain no inappropriate material. However, because of the nature of the Internet, it is impossible to guarantee that these sites will remain active indefinitely or that their contents will not be altered.